MODERN DATABASE MANAGEMENT CASEBOOK

MODERN DATABASE MANAGEMENT CASEBOOK

Weyman Whitlock
University of Florida

Klara Nelson
University of Tampa

Raymond Papp
University of Tampa

Edited by: Mary B. Prescott
University of Tampa

Upper Saddle River, New Jersey 07458

Executive editor: David Alexander
Project Manager: Lori Cerreto
Production editor: Carol Zaino
Manufacturer: Courier (Bookmart Press, Inc.)

ISBN 0-13-061191-3

10 9 8 7 6 5 4 3 2 1

CONTENTS

PREFACE

This Case Book supplements *Modern Database Management, 6th edition* by Jeffrey A. Hoffer, Mary B. Prescott, and Fred McFadden. It contains nine realistic cases that can be used as sources for projects in an introductory database course. Each case is based on a different, realistic, business model, and is scoped to serve as a student database project. The case situations are fictitious, though the collegiate basketball case directs students to data readily available on the NCAA website. There are similarities to real businesses but none of the cases represents the complete practices of an actual organization.

The cases represent a technical training school (Wright Technical Institute), a family-owned fitness center (Fit-4-Life), a small chain of medical centers (FirstCare Medical Centers), and a vineyard (LeeAnne Vineyards). Also included are a collegiate athletic database (An NCAA College Basketball Database), a bicycle manufacturer (Cellibini Mountain Bikes), a conference management system (Conference on International Business Studies(CIBS)), a flower shop (Rose Garden Flowers and Gifts), and a flower wholesaler (Westcoast Floral, Inc.).

Each case is self-contained. A set of general instructions and assignments is included that is applicable to all of the cases. The assignments may be customized to suit course objectives. The cases can be solved and implemented using any relational database product, including products such as Microsoft Access, SQLServer, or Oracle. Case notes, including comments, entity-relationship diagrams, and a relational schema for each case are available on the instructor website for *Modern Database Management*.

We wish to thank the Prentice Hall staff for their support in preparing this casebook. We are particularly grateful to the three experienced database professors who contributed the cases for this casebook. Weyman Whitlock contributed Wright Technical Institute, Fit-4-Life, FirstCare Medical Centers, and LeeAnne Vineyards, Inc. Klara Nelson revised The NCAA Data Base and Cellibini Bicycle Company from the 3rd Edition Casebook, and contributed CIBS. Raymond Papp contributed Rose Garden Flowers & Gifts and Westcoast Floral, Inc.

Mary B. Prescott

TEAM PROJECT REQUIREMENTS

INTRODUCTION

In this project your team will model an organization's data needs and will design and prototype a database application. These instructions apply to each case included in this book. The project will be divided into two phases and a presentation. The specific project deliverables required of your team for each phase and the presentation are described below.

PHASE I

1. Executive Overview

Write a 1½-2 page description of your team's initial analysis of the business scenario as it pertains to the design of a database application. Write this as though you are writing to the client for whom you are performing the analysis. You should communicate your team's vision for what the system being designed is to accomplish. Thus, describe the specific functions that your system is to perform. Be detailed. This overview should communicate to the client your understanding of what it is that you have been hired to do. If you have made any significant assumptions in your analysis that affect the design of your system, include these here. Then, *briefly* (approximately one paragraph) list and describe the other sections in this phase's deliverable package. Close the overview by *briefly* (approximately one paragraph) describing what will be done in the next phase of the project.

2. Conceptual Data Model (Entity-Relationship Diagram)

Provide a conceptual data model for your proposed system using an entity-relationship diagram. Use the notation used in your textbook. (You may use an alternative notation *only if it has been pre-approved by your instructor.*) Show all relevant entities and the relationships between these entities, including the cardinalities of the relationships and their participation types (optionalities). Attributes of the entities must be shown using the same notation as that shown in the textbook (including derived, composite, and multi-valued attributes, if any exist in your diagram). The attribute(s) that serve as the identifier for each entity must be underlined. Many-to-many relationships may be resolved into associative entities if a given situation makes such use desirable.

3. Logical Data Model (Normalized Relational Schema)

Using the graphical notation for creating a relational schema as described in your textbook, prepare a logical data model that reflects the data and relationships of this business as they would be implemented in a RDBMS based on the information presented in the ERD from the previous step. Your schema should reflect relations that are in third normal form (3NF). Make sure that the field(s) comprising the primary key of each relation is (are) underlined. Include referential integrity constraints and designations of functional dependency (using arrow notation). Use different arrow styles to clearly distinguish the referential integrity arrows from the functional dependency arrows. You should minimize the crossing of lines and avoid the overlapping of lines in your schema.

4. Data Dictionary

The data dictionary should define all fields used in the database. The format to be used is flexible, but should include such information as the field name, description, any synonyms for that field used in the system, data type, field size, format, any constraints on allowable values (e.g., validation rules or required field settings), and any other field properties (e.g., index settings) deemed necessary. (Note: It is not acceptable to use the Microsoft Access automated documentation tool.)

5. Report Designs

Identify and describe five of the most important (in your opinion) printed reports the system will need to generate. Suggestions for reports are included at the end of some of the cases. Other cases require you to infer from the body of the case. Include both a textual description and an actual report mockup for each report. The textual description should include the purpose of the report, the recipient(s) of the report, any user-definable parameters that can be used in generating the report (e.g., date range for data), any sorting/grouping/totaling used in the report, etc. The report mockup is to be a representation, typically created with a word processor, of what the report will look like. Sample data is to be used to show where actual data will be displayed on the printed page. Include an adequate amount of data to demonstrate the report features. Headers, footers, and totals are to be shown where applicable. These preliminary report designs should help you verify that the database design being proposed is adequate to provide all necessary information. (The final report designs in the Phase II prototype may differ somewhat in actual appearance from these designs. Also, additional reports will surely be desirable for inclusion in Phase II.)

PHASE II

1. Application Prototype

For the software application, you are to create a working relational database prototype using a database engine approved by your instructor. Your prototype should demonstrate your implementation of the work you submitted in the previous phase (incorporating any changes necessary based on any corrections made to the earlier work). Your application must include *at least* 50 sample records in the largest table and an appropriate amount of test data in each of the other tables. You should demonstrate your command of tables, queries, forms, and reports. If you use Microsoft Access you should also use macros appropriately. (VBA modules may be included if you desire, but this is *not* a requirement.) You are encouraged to make your prototype as attractive and professional in appearance and operation as possible. Be creative and ambitious! However, it is better to have a modest application that is well designed and works reliably than a flashy one that has flaws and experiences errors. A working copy of the prototype must be submitted with the documentation package (see below).

2.   Documentation

A detailed, printed user manual must accompany the prototype. The user manual should be designed to provide a novice system user with all the information necessary to successfully use the application to perform all the functions for which it was designed. A very high level of professionalism is expected in the preparation of this document. The user manual should include "screen shots" from your application where useful and should include an appendix that contains sample outputs of all reports. (You may assume that the future users of the system are familiar with Microsoft Windows.) All figures that display screen shots should reference the database program that is shown in the screen shot.

PRESENTATION

Each team will present their completed prototype to the class. In addition to database programs approved by your instructor, teams may make brief use of Microsoft PowerPoint. Your instructor will indicate the length of your presentation. Each member of the team should demonstrate his or her ability to give a professional presentation. All students must verbally participate in their team's presentation. Typically, groups simulate a presentation to the potential buyers and/or users of the application.

CASE A — Wright Technical Institute

INTRODUCTION

In 1991, Richard Wright and his wife Eliza founded Wright Technical Institute (WTI) in Mishawaka, Indiana. Theirs was the first computer software training business in the area and was immediately successful. Over the decade since its inception, WTI has grown steadily and is still the market leader in computer training in the Mishawaka area. The growth of the company has caused bookkeeping problems for the Wrights who, up until the present, have kept all their business records in a series of Microsoft Excel spreadsheets. The Wrights have decided to address the inadequacy of the current system by instituting the use of a database system to be created with Microsoft Access. The Wrights have also decided that they are too busy running the day-to-day operations of their business to design the database system themselves, so they have decided to request proposals from several local software development companies that specialize in custom database system development. As members of one of these companies, you and your consulting team will prepare a design proposal and prototype for the database system for WTI. A member of your company has already completed an initial business analysis, and the results of that study follow below.

FACILITIES AND PERSONNEL

WTI occupies a suite of large office spaces in a modern office building in downtown Mishawaka. Some of the office space is used for administrative purposes and storage, but most of it has been renovated into eight computer-training classrooms (numbered 1 through 8) in which the classes offered by WTI are taught. The capacity, in students, of the classrooms ranges from 10 for the smallest room up to 18 for the largest of the rooms. The classrooms also vary in the type of computers installed in them. One of the medium-sized rooms contains Apple Macintosh computers. All of the other rooms contain IBM-compatible computers. Of these rooms, most have Pentium-class machines, but two of the smallest still have older 486-class machines. Half of the classrooms (the Macintosh room and three of the Pentium rooms) also are wired for direct Internet connections to allow for classes that require such connectivity (e.g., for offerings of the Introduction to the Internet course).

WTI currently employs 10 full-time trainers. One of the trainers has been with WTI since it opened, and another has been with the company for five years, but the others have been around for much shorter periods of time. (Through the company's history, a trainer typically stays with WTI for around two to three years.) When hired, each trainer is issued an employee number. This is actually a nine-digit code comprised of eight digits specifying the year, month, and day an employee was hired, followed by one additional digit to allow for coding multiple hires on the same date. (For example, the first employee hired on December 1, 1998 would have the employee number 199812011.) Information also recorded by WTI on each trainer, in addition to the employee number, includes the employee's name (first and last), address (street, city, state, and zip), phone number, and e-mail address.

Trainers must, obviously, learn a course's material before they can teach a class in that course. Trainers are typically given one day per week to study new course materials. (However, newly hired trainers get the first two weeks of their employment to study for their first teaching assignments.) Richard always attempts to have at least two trainers qualified to teach every course (although this may temporarily not be the case for newly developed classes). This provides flexibility in scheduling classes and trainers. When Richard feels that a trainer is familiar enough with the course material to teach a class in a given course, he notes the trainer, the course, and the date of qualification in one of his spreadsheets. From this list he can determine which trainers are qualified to teach which classes.

COURSE OFFERINGS AND SUPPORTING MATERIALS

The courses themselves are identified by a 10-character code specified by Richard for each course. (For example, WINXPINTRO for the course, Introduction to Windows XP.) Most courses are one day in length, although some are two or three days, and a few are five days. The fee charged to attend a class varies depending on the course. The more technical courses (e.g., Advanced Novell Networking) are more expensive than introductory courses and, of course, multi-day courses are more expensive than single-day courses. It is also important to note what hardware requirements a course has. For instance, some courses require Macintosh computers while most require IBM-compatible machines. Among the latter, some require Pentium-class machines, while others can be conducted on 486-based computers. Although classes in most courses can be taken by anyone at any time, some courses are advanced enough that they have WTI prerequisites. That is, before a client may enroll for some of WTI's offerings, they must complete one or more prerequisite courses. (And some courses with prerequisites are themselves prerequisites for one or more other courses.)

The specific software programs used in the courses vary. Some courses (e.g., Introduction to Microsoft Office 2000) utilize several programs (e.g., Word, Excel, PowerPoint, etc.) while others (e.g., Advanced Microsoft Word 2000) require only one. Each software program has been given an eight-character code to identify it (e.g., MSWORD00). The name of the software program and its publisher are also recorded. The operating system that the program requires to run (e.g., Windows 2000) is also recorded. The number of licenses that WTI owns for each program is also important to track. (This number represents the maximum number of copies of a particular program that can be in actual use by WTI at any given moment in time.)

Another important component of the courses offered by WTI is the course book that is selected by Eliza for use in each course. The fee charged each client for each course includes one copy of the course book. Eliza selects books from those available from a number of different publishers. She receives catalogs from these publishers listing all their computer-related book offerings. For each course that WTI offers, Eliza selects one book. No two courses use the same book. She keeps records (in an Excel spreadsheet, as usual) of the books she selects that include the International Standard Book Number (ISBN), book title, author name(s), publisher, and list price. Although Eliza has developed preferences for certain authors and publishers, she also records information on other books that she intends to review for possible future ordering. She orders her selected books from a variety of book vendors (each with a unique name). All of the books she orders are popular titles available from any of the vendors. Some orders she places by phone; others, she places by mail. For each order she places, Eliza assigns a sequential order number and records the date that the order was placed. A typical book order will contain anywhere from one to 10 different titles. Since she attempts to keep WTI's on-hand inventory of books to a minimum, she orders specific titles in small quantities, and orders daily. Most orders are delivered within one or two days. Eliza keeps track of the status of each order by noting whether it is open (undelivered) or closed (delivered). Orders are always filled with a single delivery; that is, there are no back orders. (Books that are shorted are simply ordered from a secondary vendor.) For all orders, Eliza records the quantity of each book on the order and the actual price charged per book by the vendor. (There are occasional differences in the price charged by a vendor for a book compared to the publisher's list price.)

CLIENT MEMBERSHIPS AND CLASS ENROLLMENTS

The core of WTI's business, of course, is the enrollment of clients for classes offered by the company. WTI offers classes representing over 30 different courses to its clients. It publishes a schedule of class offerings each month that it mails out to clients who have attended at least one class in the last six months. A listing for a specific class offering includes information on the course taught in the class, the trainer, the room, and the start date. For identification purposes, each scheduled class is also assigned a unique, five-digit, sequential reference number. Eliza is in charge of marketing efforts and carefully records information on WTI's clients. Each client is assigned a unique, six-digit, sequential client number. The client's name (first and last), address (street, city, state, and zip), and phone are recorded. Additionally, the initial date that a client enrolls for a WTI course is also recorded. (Eliza does this to facilitate marketing mailings of the "Happy 1st Anniversary as a WTI Client" variety.) Since enrollment requests for some of WTI classes may exceed the capacity of the class, Eliza records the date and time that a client requests to enroll in a particular class. Since she knows how many students can be accommodated for a given class, she is able to inform the client immediately if they are confirmed for the class, or if they must be placed on a waiting list. If they are placed on a waiting list, then they may be accepted for a class if other clients cancel their enrollment. The date & time of enrollment request determines the order in which clients on the waiting list are added to a class. If the client is not placed on a waiting list, then immediate full payment for the class is required, and the amount recorded.

Although each course has a predetermined fee, the actual amount that a client pays for attending a class varies depending on what membership type the client has. Each client, when they first seek to enroll in a WTI course, is required to choose a membership type. Each membership type is identified by a single-letter code. Additional information associated with each membership type is the price of the membership, the duration (in days) that the membership is good for, and the discount applied to the fee charged for any classes enrolled in by the client. For example, a client that chooses the annual discount plan (code A) pays $300 a year for membership, but then receives a 30% discount off the regular fee they would otherwise pay for any class for an entire year. A similar semi-annual plan (code S) costs $200 and also provides a 30% discount. There is also a regular membership (code R) that lasts one year and has no charge but provides no discount, and the employee family membership (code E) which is available to members of an employee's immediate family and that lasts one year with a 25% discount. (Additional membership types are in the process of being set up, but have not been sold to any client yet.) A client may renew or change membership types at the end of any membership period. When a client is assigned to a membership type, the date of the assignment is recorded as well as the amount of payment made.

CONCLUSION

The Wrights have high hopes for their anticipated database system. In addition to duplicating the abilities of the existing system, they are optimistic that your experience in database analysis and design will provide you with the insight necessary to identify other possible benefits to WTI of a well-designed relational database system. You and your team look forward to the challenge of delivering such a system to Wright Technical Institute.

CASE B Fit-4-Life Fitness Center

INTRODUCTION

In 1996, Arnold and Maria Starks opened the Fit-4-Life Fitness Center in Cocoa Beach, Florida. This business was the culmination of a dream of the Starks to open their own health and fitness business, after having worked in this industry for others for several years. As husband and wife, Arnold and Maria have thoroughly enjoyed the opportunity to work together over the last five years in building a successful family business.

Fit-4-Life is somewhat different than many other businesses in the personal fitness industry in that it is not simply a gymnasium facility stocked with exercise equipment for use by paying customers. Instead, the Starks' business plan was to create a learning center that emphasized offering classes on fitness techniques and skills that could be learned by patrons from trained instructors. The fees paid by members of the center for these classes make up the largest of the three sources of revenue for the business. Another revenue source is the initial membership fee paid by center members upon joining Fit-4-Life. The other revenue source is the sale of fitness supplies in the store located in the center. This store carries both fitness clothing (e.g., work-out suits, sweat bands, etc.) and also nutritional supplements (e.g., vitamins, protein powders, etc.).

As the business has grown and developed, Arnold and Maria have found that the volume of paperwork associated with running the business has also substantially increased, and has become very difficult to properly maintain. They are concerned that their business will not be able to successfully continue growing without a more timely and accurate means of maintaining the records of the business. This realization has led them to decide that the adoption of a computer-based record keeping system is in their best interests. They have invited several system development consulting firms, including yours, to visit them to discuss their business needs, and to propose an automated solution. They will review the proposed solutions from the competing consulting firms and will ultimately select one firm to develop and implement their final system.

A systems analyst with your consulting firm has already conducted an initial interview with the Starks and has provided the information contained below on the Fit-4-Life Fitness Center. You and the other members of your consulting group will take this information and go forward with your plan for presenting the Starks with a system solution that you hope will win their approval.

PERSONNEL

In addition to Arnold and Maria Starks, Fit-4-Life employs a number of other employees, primarily as fitness course instructors. Other positions filled by employees include the clerks in the fitness store and administrative personnel (e.g., billing clerks, equipment managers, etc.). Records on each past and present employee of the company are maintained that include the employee name, address, phone number, hire date, position, and status as either a current or former employee. Employees also have a unique sequential four-digit Employee ID number assigned to them when they are originally hired. (Payroll is currently outsourced to an accounting firm. This is expected to continue and will not be a part of the system to be developed.)

MEMBERS

Information is also recorded for members of the Fit-4-Life Fitness Center also have information recorded on them, of course. When joining the center, individuals have a unique sequential six-digit Member ID number assigned to them. Also recorded for each member is his or her name, address, phone number, gender, birth date, and date of joining Fit-4-Life (which allows anniversary marketing letters).

Each member, when originally joining, decides on one of four available membership types: Platinum, Gold, Silver, and Bronze. Each of these membership types has a fixed joining fee associated with it. These fees, in descending order from Platinum to Bronze membership types are $500, $300, $100, and $10. This is a one-time fee that establishes a lifetime membership in the center.

The reason for the varying joining fees is that each membership type also has an associated discount percentage associated with it. This is a percentage amount that the member will have deducted from all their future expenditures at the center, applied to both course enrollments and purchases in the center store. The specific discount percentages, in descending order from Platinum to Bronze membership types are 30%, 20%, 10%, and 0%. Thus, the joining member chooses a membership type (and its related joining fee) based on their expectation of the value of the discounts to be received from their purchases in the future. (E.g., a member expecting to take many courses and/or purchase many items from the center store would have incentive to purchase one of the more expensive membership types.)

 As an incentive to get new members to initially purchase the highest priced memberships possible, Fit-4-Life does not allow upgrades to the membership type once purchased. (A member wishing to purchase a higher membership type must rejoin, paying a full joining fee and being assigned a new Membership ID.)

FITNESS COURSES

Fit-4-Life offers over thirty different personal fitness courses to its members. Courses include such exercise-based subjects as yoga, tai chi, weight training, and aerobics, and also other fitness-oriented topics such as nutrition and natural medicine. All courses are taught by Fit-4-Life instructors.

Before teaching a course offering, an instructor employee of Fit-4-Life must first qualify to teach the course. Both Arnold and Maria Starks are experts in all subject matter taught at Fit-4-Life and are the judges of when an instructor is qualified to teach a course. The date that an instructor qualifies for teaching a particular course is recorded by the Starks.

Each course has a unique course number assigned to it when it is created. The course number consists of three letters followed by three digits (e.g., AER101 for Introduction to Aerobics). Additional important information about each course is the course name, description, category (e.g., novice, intermediate, advanced), duration (the number of weeks that the course is designed to run), and fee (the price of the course, prior to any applied discounts). There are no prerequisites, as such, for taking courses, but members are encouraged to take courses in a logical progression (e.g., novice classes prior to intermediate classes in a particular subject area).

Courses are offered periodically in the form of classes. (A class is a specific offering of a course.) Each class has a unique identifying number called a Reference No. This is a five-digit sequential number (e.g., 00256) that is assigned to a course offering when it is placed on the center teaching schedule. Also recorded on the teaching schedule for each class is the start date for the class, the day(s) of the week the class will be held (e.g., M, MWF, TR, etc.), the time period that the class will be held (e.g., 8:00am-10:00am, 7:30pm-9:00pm, etc.), and the instructor. Classroom assignment must also be recorded. The center has seven rooms that are used for classes. (See below.)

FACILITIES AND EQUIPMENT

Each room at the center has a unique sequential room number and a class capacity associated with it. The latter is the maximum number of members that can participate in a class being held in that room. This number is important in preventing classes from being overenrolled.

Some of the rooms at the center contain pieces of exercise equipment. Each such piece of equipment has a unique serial number (provided by its manufacturer) that is used to track it in the center. Also recorded for each piece are its purchase date and the date of its last maintenance. (All equipment at the center is routinely inspected and refurbished on a routine schedule.) Each piece of equipment belongs to a specific equipment type. (E.g., the center might own five different StairMaster 5000 machines, each having a unique serial number, all considered to be a single equipment type.) Each equipment type is assigned a unique sequential three-digit identification number. Also recorded for each type are its description, the manufacturer's model number, and the recommended mainte-nance interval for that model of equipment. Some courses require the use of a particular type of equipment, and that need must be accommodated when scheduling classes. (No course requires the use of more than one type of equipment, however.)

To facilitate the maintenance of the equipment, information on the manufacturer of the equipment is maintained. (Due to warranty requirements, the maintenance of the equipment is performed exclusively by the manufacturer of the equipment.) Each equipment type is associated with a single manufacturer. Each manufacturer is referenced by an assigned unique sequential two-digit manufacturer ID number. Additional information maintained on each manufacturer is the company name, address, phone number, and fax number. When maintenance is required on a piece of equipment, a work order is generated. Each such work order is given a unique sequential five-digit number. Also recorded for each work order is the date of the order, the serial number of the piece of equipment involved, the manufacturer performing the maintenance, and (when the work is

completed) the amount charged for the work. Each piece of
equipment being worked on requires a separate work order.

MERCHANDISE SALES

As mentioned earlier, Fit-4-Life also maintains an in-center store for
the sale of merchandise to members. The items for sale in the store
are each identified by a unique item ID (e.g., VIT-1342, SWB-0224,
etc.). Also recorded for each item is its description, standard price
(the price before any applicable member discounts), the quantity on
hand (inventory amount), and the reorder point. This latter quantity is
the minimum quantity of the item that should be kept on hand. If an
item's inventory level falls below this point, the item is noted for
reorder from the vendor that supplies it. (All items have only a single
source.)

The vendors of the items also have information recorded about them.
Each is assigned a unique sequential two-digit ID number. Also
recorded is each vendor's company name, address, phone number,
and fax number.

A supply order is placed with each vendor periodically (typically
around once a week for most vendors). Each such order is assigned
a unique order number by Fit-4-Life. A specific format is used for
order numbers. An order number is a combination of the two-digit
vendor number, and an additional sequential five-digit number (e.g.,
12-12387). The date the order is placed is also recorded, as is the
date that the order is received. (No backordering of merchandise is
accepted by the center, so there is only one date received for each
order placed.) The specific item(s) ordered, the quantity ordered of
each item, the quantity received of each item, and the cost charged by
the vendor per unit of each item are recorded for each order. Also
noted is the employee placing the order. The overall order total cost
is also calculated for each order.

Whenever a Fit-4-Life member comes into the store and purchases
one or more items, a unique sequential seven-digit transaction

number is generated (e.g., 0003456). The member making the purchase and the date of the transaction are also recorded. Of course, the specific items purchased, along with the quantity of each item, and the price per unit of each item, are also necessarily recorded. (The unit price charged for an item must reflect any discount from the item's standard price to which the purchaser's membership type entitles them.) The employee making the sale is also noted. The overall purchase total is also calculated for each transaction.

CONCLUSION

The Starks are optimistic that a well-designed database system will substantially improve their business processes. They are depending on you to analyze their business to identify areas that can benefit from such a system, and to design and develop the system itself. They have promised to work closely with you and to provide full support in the development process. You and your team are excited at the prospect of undertaking this challenge.

CASE C

FirstCare Medical Centers

INTRODUCTION

Dr. Robert Slate is the owner and President of FirstCare Medical Centers, Inc., a small chain of medical centers located in Alcoa, a medium-sized city in the Florida panhandle. The company was originally founded as a single center and has expanded to its current size of four centers in only five years. Dr. Slate grew up working in his father's business, a retail pharmacy, and developed an interest in the healthcare field at an early age. He majored in Medicine in college and, after graduation, worked in a variety of medical settings. Eventually, he returned to school to earn his MBA degree, with an eye towards establishing his own medical business.

Five years ago he opened the original FirstCare center. He believed that there was a market niche for the type of services offered at FirstCare. The centers are for people who need occasional medical care but are without a regular family physician. The centers fill a middle ground between traditional family physician practices and hospital emergency rooms. Most of the patients treated at FirstCare make advance appointments to be seen at a center. Walk-in patients are also accepted if there are available appointment slots. The centers are open from 9 a.m. to 7 p.m., Monday through Friday, and are closed on weekends and holidays.

FACILITIES AND PERSONNEL

Each of the four FirstCare centers has a unique Center ID number (1, 2, 3, or 4) assigned to it. All centers also have a name (e.g., Horizon Hills FirstCare Medical Center), address, and phone number. Each FirstCare center is managed by one administrative employee.

Each of the centers employs a number of personnel. Each employee falls into one of three distinct categories: administrative workers (e.g., managers, clerks, receptionists, etc.), nurses, and pharmacists. The company records several pieces of information about all of its employees: social security number (which serves as an identification number), name (first name, middle initial, and last name), address, phone number, and the center at which the employee works. No employee works at more than one center.

Specific additional information is recorded for employees in each of the personnel categories. Administrative personnel have their job title recorded. Nurses and pharmacists have both their license number and license expiration date recorded. The license numbers are assigned by the Department of Professional Regulation (DPR) and are codes that begin with two letters ("PS" for pharmacists and "RN" for nurses) followed by seven digits, which are sequentially assigned to each new licensee in the state. For example, a pharmacist license number could be PS0017038. Nurse and pharmacist licenses must be renewed every two years and FirstCare keeps track of the expiration dates in order to make sure that none of the nurses or pharmacists neglects to renew their license on time.

In addition to these FirstCare employees, the company also requires the services of contract physicians. These doctors are not considered employees of FirstCare, but rather are paid as independent contractors to provide medical services at the four FirstCare centers. The company records information on these physicians, including their name (first name and last name), pager number, and specialty (e.g., cardiology, orthopedics, etc.). A physician may have more than one specialty.

Each physician is uniquely identified by his or her DEA Number. This is a letter-number combination (e.g., AW1234563) that is assigned to licensed physicians by the federal Drug Enforcement Administration. The identifier always consists of two letters followed by seven numbers. The first letter is always "A" or "B" and the second letter is always the first letter of the physician's last name.

These doctors are scheduled in advance to serve at the various clinics. They are not assigned exclusively to a single center, but may be assigned to different centers on different days, as demand requires. They may even, in fact, be assigned to one center for part of a day and another center for another part of the same day. Thus, the company needs to keep track of which physicians work at which centers on which days and the start time and end time for each assignment.

PATIENTS AND PATIENT APPOINTMENTS

The patients seen at the FirstCare centers must have information recorded about them, and about the appointments that they make to be seen for care. Each patient, upon their first visit, patients are assigned a unique six-digit Patient ID number (e.g., 100312). This number uses the first digit to indicate at which of the FirstCare centers (1, 2, 3, or 4) the patient was first seen. The remaining digits are assigned sequentially.

Patients can make appointments at different centers, but their Patient ID number never changes, once assigned. Also recorded for all patients are their name (first name and last name), address, phone number, and insurance status (yes or no). Although all transactions with FirstCare are paid for directly by the patient, if the patient has an insurance status of "yes" then the FirstCare personnel know to fill out special detailed receipts that the patient can then use to place a claim for reimbursement with their insurance company.

When a patient calls for an appointment or is accepted for a "walk-in" visit without a previously scheduled appointment, a unique seven-digit Appointment ID (e.g., 2003919) is assigned. This number uses the first digit to indicate at which of the FirstCare centers (1, 2, 3, or 4) the appointment is made. The remaining digits are assigned sequentially. The date and time of the appointment are also recorded, as is the patient's stated reason for making the appointment and the specific physician assigned to this appointment.

Additionally, the fee charged for the appointment is recorded. The typical fixed fee for a FirstCare appointment is $35. In rare circumstances, such as particularly difficult or lengthy care situations, the center manager may increase this fee for a given appointment. All appointment fees are the direct responsibility of the patient. FirstCare provides a receipt for the amount paid that patients with health care insurance can submit to their insurer for reimbursement.

Appointments are typically scheduled for each doctor in half-hour blocks. Although most appointments require no more than half this amount of time, this scheduling allows for the occasional lengthy appointment, as well as allowing paperwork to be taken care of between patients.

PHARMACEUTICAL SERVICES

In addition to the care provided to the patients by the contract physicians and employee nurses, FirstCare also provides pharmaceutical services. Each center operates a pharmacy in the same building as the clinic facilities. FirstCare employs licensed pharmacists to fill prescriptions for its patients in these pharmacies. These on-site pharmacies provide a convenience for the FirstCare patients, and provide additional profits to the company as well.

Only prescriptions written by FirstCare physicians for FirstCare patients are filled at these pharmacies. This allows the pharmacies to maintain a relatively restricted inventory of medications, as they can tailor their stock to the drugs of choice of the physicians contracted with by the centers. However, patients can fill their prescriptions at pharmacies not affiliated with FirstCare if they prefer. Although the pharmacies carry some medications that do not legally require a prescription to purchase, such as topical antibacterial creams, company policy requires that all medications dispensed from a FirstCare pharmacy to a patient have a prescription order by one of the FirstCare physicians.

Each new order is assigned a unique prescription number. This number actually begins with a letter signifying which of the center pharmacies filled the prescription (A is used by the first center, B by the second center, etc.) followed by a five-digit sequential number that originally began at each center with 00001 and is incremented (e.g., A00002, A00003, etc.) for each new prescription filled. Each prescription indicates which physician wrote it and the name of the patient for whom the medication is intended. The medication itself is, of course, specified on the prescription, as is the quantity to be dispensed and the instructions for use. It is also necessary to record which pharmacist filled the prescription and the price charged for it.

For medications that legally require a prescription, the price is calculated as the wholesale cost of the medication plus a $3.00 dispensing fee. For medications that do not legally require a prescription (so called "over the counter", or OTC drugs), the price is wholesale cost plus 30 percent.

Another company policy forbids refills of FirstCare prescriptions. If a patient has a chronic condition requiring ongoing treatment, FirstCare believes that they should establish a traditional relationship with a regular physician, rather than using the FirstCare model of health care. Thus, a given prescription can only be filled once. Should a FirstCare physician desire to provide more of the same medication to the same patient, perhaps on a subsequent visit, they must write another prescription.

The drug inventory at each FirstCare pharmacy must also be properly tracked. Each drug, both prescription and non-prescription, is uniquely identifiable by a National Drug Code (NDC) number. This is a number assigned by drug manufacturers that follows a standard format: five digits comprising a manufacturer code, a dash, four digits comprising a product code, another dash, and two digits comprising a package code. For example, Amoxil's code is 00029-6006-30 for a bottle of one hundred 250mg in capsules.

Other facts maintained for each medication item are: drug name/strength, package quantity, unit (e.g., tablet, gram, milliliter, etc.), and average wholesale price (AWP) per package size. The AWP for all drugs is readily obtainable from published catalogs. Although small differences in pricing exist between wholesalers, AWP is commonly used as a pricing basis.

Each drug's legal class is also recorded. The possibilities for class are:
- non-prescription (OTC),
- prescription only (also called legend drugs or Rx)
- controlled substance (a class which is subdivided into four separate subclasses: CII, CIII, CIV, and CV, in decreasing order of addictive potential).

Lastly, each drug's principal therapeutic use (e.g., antibiotic, analgesic, antihypertensive, etc.) is listed. This is primarily recorded in order to do sales analyses of drug movement by category of use.

In addition, the pharmacists in each store are responsible for determining the minimum stock levels that should be maintained for each drug item based on their knowledge of their customer's needs and seasonal variations. The actual quantity on hand of each drug item is currently estimated; an accurate inventory is desirable to facilitate timely reordering.
A listing of sample drug product data is shown in Figure 1 at the end of the case.

Each patient's prescription history is recorded using patient prescription profile cards. These are 8½" by 11" cards, kept in a counter-top file box, arranged alphabetically. These must be updated each time a prescription is filled or any other information about the patient changes, so that the pharmacist knows how often the patient has received certain medications and what other drugs are being prescribed for the patient, to allow the pharmacist to check for potential drug interactions. A copy of a patient profile card is shown in Figure 2 at the end of the case.

The typical procedure for the filling of a prescription is as follows:

- Verify the patient's name and address written on the prescription order when presented by the patient.
- Retrieve the patient's prescription profile card or prepare a new card if patient is new.
- Type the prescription bottle label.
- Get the product from the shelf.
- Put the appropriate amount in the patient's bottle.
- Use a numbering stamp machine to assign a sequential prescription number which must be posted on the patient profile card, the prescription order form, and the label on the prescription bottle.
- Price the prescription.
- Record the prescription information and price on the patient profile, the daily transaction log (a listing of data on all prescriptions filled that day), the prescription receipt, and the prescription order form.
- (In addition to the simpler payment receipt, prepare an insurance claim form for those customers who have prescription insurance coverage. About 30% of the customers have health insurance that covers prescriptions; the patients pay cash for their prescriptions and then submit the standard claim form to their insurer for reimbursement.
- Re-file the patient profile card alphabetically.
- File the prescription order form numerically.
- Present prescription to patient and collect payment for it.

If the prescription is for a controlled substance, additional paperwork must be done. The prescription order must be marked with a red "C" letter stamp and the dispensing information (Rx number, drug name, strength, and quantity dispensed) must be entered into a controlled substances daily log form so that pharmacy inspectors from the DPR and DEA are able to determine what, and how many, controlled substance prescriptions are filled on a daily basis.

Additionally, the pharmacist must flag the drug for re-order if the quantity on the shelf is below the minimum stock level for that item and post the drug NDC number and quantity of packages desired in the order book, a loose leaf notebook. The orders are then phoned in to a drug wholesaler at the end of each day. Each such order is assigned a unique order number, which is formulated as the center number, a dash, and a four-digit sequential number. (For example, 2-0187.) In addition to the order number, also recorded are the date the order was placed and the Vendor ID of the wholesaler with which the order was placed.

When the order arrives, the date of arrival is recorded. The number of packages of each drug received is also recorded. The number of packages received may or may not be the same as the quantity ordered. The actual package cost of each drug received, which likely will not be identical to the AWP cost used in formulating patient prescription pricing, is likewise recorded. The total order cost, which is the sum of all individual item totals on the order, is also recorded. There is no shipping charge or sales tax.

There is one preferred vendor, Johnson Drug Company, but two other vendors are used when the preferred vendor either doesn't carry an item or is out of stock. In no event is any part of a drug order backordered. That is, there is only one shipment per order. Any shorted items must be obtained with another order, possibly with a secondary vendor if the drug is needed quickly. Each of the vendors utilized is assigned a unique, sequential, Vendor ID number (e.g., 1, 2, 3). Also recorded for each vendor is: company name, address, phone number, and fax number.

CLIENT COMMENTS

As the size of his business has increased, Dr. Slate has reassessed the way in which his centers do business. The amount of information that must be acquired and processed has been steadily growing, partly due to management needs to track business trends and expenses, and partly due to increasing insurance company and government reporting requirements. It has become very difficult to keep up with these information demands using the old manual systems that have been in place since the company was founded. He believes the time to automate has come. Dr. Slate has identified much of the information that an automated system will need to track, in his opinion. He has suggested a number of functions that would be desirable for the proposed system to perform:

- Maintain personnel information on all doctors and employees affiliated with FirstCare
- Track physician work assignments at the individual centers and print a weekly schedule for each doctor
- Track patient appointments and print daily appointment schedules for use by each of the centers
- Track total revenues generated by medical care appointments, by time period
- Track total revenues generated by pharmacy sales, by time period
- Track total expenditures for items purchased from wholesale vendors, by time period
- Provide online, and be able to print, all the information currently provided by the patient profile cards
- Provide customers, upon request, with itemized yearly lists of medical care (appointment) expenses and also prescription purchases, for income tax reporting purposes
- Enable direct mail marketing of targeted patients (e.g., form letters created to offer discounts to diabetic patients as identified by the type of prescription drugs dispensed to them)
- Automatically generate prescription numbers and prices, and record all information associated with the filling of prescription orders
- Generate prescription labels and patient receipts for the medications dispensed
- Generate detailed customer receipts (appointment or prescription) for insurance claims when applicable
- Generate a daily dispensed drug log and a separate log of dispensed controlled substances, which must be kept to meet DPR and DEA requirements
- Generate drug re-order reports for items that have fallen below their minimum stock amounts
- Help prevent pharmacist and nurse licenses from expiring without being noticed

- Track drug movement by category and by time period to improve inventory control
- Provide total itemized inventory in stock by quantity and total valuation for inventory tax purposes

He recognizes that other opportunities for automation may also exist and is ready and willing to depend on the expertise of the system designers to identify such other opportunities. However, Dr. Slate also recognizes that the initial implementation of his new automated system may not provide 100% of his desired objectives. He is optimistic, though, that the majority of his needs will be met by the system as initially delivered.

Dr. Slate desires that the system be able to print patient profile cards and prescription labels in exactly the same format as currently being used. However, he has no such constraints on any other printed materials and wishes to leave the design of these documents to the professional skills of the system designers.

Dr. Slate currently utilizes an outside accounting firm to handle his payroll, accounts payable, and all other financial transactions and does not need the proposed database system to handle these areas at this time. Additionally, he has stated that purchases of non-pharmacy supplies (e.g., soap, towels, office supplies, etc.) do not need to be dealt with at this time.

CONCLUSION

Dr. Slate is hopeful that a database system can be developed by you and your team to automate his outdated manual system. He is optimistic that such a system will provide many benefits to his current business and will facilitate its future growth. You and your team are determined to make his vision of this system a reality.

Figure 1: Sample Drug Product Data

NDC Number	Name/Strength	Size	Units	Price	Class	Use
00006-0516-68	Aldomet 500mg	100	Tab	67.44	Rx	Antihypertensive
00378-0137-01	Allopurinol 100mg	100	Tab	9.17	Rx	Uricosuric
00093-3111-10	Ampicillin 250mg	1000	Cap	125.80	Rx	Antibiotic
00008-0064-03	Ativan 1mg	500	Tab	431.34	CIV	Antianxiety
00029-6074-47	Augmentin 250mg Chewable	30	Tab	59.52	Rx	Antibiotic
45802-0275-03	Bacitracin/Polymyxin Oint	30	GM	2.38	OTC	Topical Anti-infective
00472-0370-15	Betamethasone 0.1% Cream	15	GM	2.91	Rx	Topical Anti-inflammatory
00074-2586-60	Biaxin 500mg	60	Tab	195.61	Rx	Antibiotic
11980-0022-05	Blephamide Ophthalmic 0.2%	5	ML	22.40	Rx	Ophth. Anti-inflammatory
00028-0105-01	Brethine 5mg	100	Tab	39.57	Rx	Bronchodilator
00003-0452-50	Capoten 25mg	100	Tab	80.95	Rx	Antihypertensive
00002-3061-02	Ceclor 250mg	100	Cap	224.20	Rx	Antibiotic
00002-5058-68	Ceclor 250mg/5ml Susp.	150	ML	56.40	Rx	Antibiotic
00085-0458-03	Claritin 10mg	100	Tab	199.14	Rx	Antihistamine
00054-4156-25	Codeine Sulfate 30mg	100	Tab	29.36	CII	Analgesic
00007-3362-03	Compazine 25mg Suppository	12	Supp	37.81	Rx	Antiemetic
00007-3366-20	Compazine 5mg	100	Tab	61.43	Rx	Antiemetic
00002-0363-03	Darvocet-N 100mg	500	Tab	288.58	CIV	Analgesic
00006-0041-68	Decadron 0.5mg	100	Tab	55.95	Rx	Anti-inflamatory
00024-0335-04	Demerol 50mg	100	Tab	75.52	CII	Analgesic
00039-0052-50	Diabeta 5mg	500	Tab	252.29	Rx	Antidiabetic
00228-2053-10	Diazepam 10mg	100	Tab	17.29	CIV	Antianxiety
00031-2230-12	Dimetapp Elixir	120	ML	4.75	OTC	Antihist./Decongestant
00044-0208-05	E-Mycin 333mg	500	Tab	153.87	Rx	Antibiotic
00364-0514-02	Furosemide 40mg	1000	Tab	45.00	Rx	Diuretic
00045-0242-60	Haldol 2mg	100	Tab	95.38	Rx	Antipsychotic
50458-0510-10	Hismanal 10mg	100	Tab	195.78	Rx	Antihistamine
00172-2089-60	Hydrochlorothiazide 50mg	100	Tab	4.23	Rx	Diuretic
00781-7017-24	Hydrocortisone 0.5% Cream	30	GM	1.95	OTC	Topical Anti-inflammatory
00046-0424-81	Inderal 40mg	100	Tab	66.11	Rx	Antihypertensive
00006-0150-30	Indocin 50mg	30	Cap	50.10	Rx	Anti-inflammatory
00777-0871-02	Keflex 500mg	100	Cap	282.61	Rx	Antibiotic
00173-0249-75	Lanoxin 0.25mg	1000	Tab	127.73	Rx	Cardiac Glycoside
00039-0060-13	Lasix 40mg	100	Tab	22.85	Rx	Diuretic
00140-0002-01	Librium 10mg	100	Cap	53.71	CIV	Antianxiety
00009-0056-02	Medrol 4mg	100	Tab	70.71	Rx	Anti-inflammatory
00781-6130-16	Paregoric Elixir	480	ML	9.25	CIII	Analgesic

Figure 2: Patient Profile Form

```
┌─────────────────────────────────────────────────────────────────────┐
│ ──────────── FIRSTCARE MEDICAL CENTERS  -  PATIENT PROFILE ───────── │
├─────────────────────────────────────────────────────────────────────┤
│ PATIENT ID: _____      Insured? _____          FirstCare         │
│ Patient Last Name: _____         Medical           │
│ Patient First Name: _____         Centers           │
├─────────────────────────────────────────────────────────────────────┤
│ Address: _____                           │
│ City/State/Zip: _____                           │
│ Telephone _____                           │
├─────────────────────────────────────────────────────────────────────┤
│ ───────────── PRESCRIPTION MEDICATION RECORD ──────────────           │
└─────────────────────────────────────────────────────────────────────┘
```

RX NUMBER	MEDICATION NAME/STRENGTH	QTY	DOCTOR	DATE	PRICE

CASE D

LeeAnne Vineyards

INTRODUCTION

In 1992, Lee and Anne Woods left behind careers in law and accounting, respectively, to pursue their dream of growing grapes and making wine. They moved to Mendocino County in California and purchased 25 acres of grape-growing land and a small winery and house. They called their new venture LeeAnne Vineyards and released their first wine for sale in 1994. They have been successful enough to gradually expand their land holdings and to increase the quantity and variety of the wines they sell.

In fact, the expansion of their business has led the Woods to consider automating the record keeping of their business with a computer database. They have invited several database consulting companies, including yours, to send in teams of analysts and developers to evaluate their business needs and to propose an automated solution to the record keeping problems brought on by the company's continued growth. The results of the preliminary investigation recently conducted by an analyst from your company are presented below.

PERSONNEL

LeeAnne Vineyards, Inc. (LVI) currently employs over two dozen full-time employees, with positions ranging from clerks to grape farmers to wine makers. Among the employees, supervisors have been appointed that oversee the work of other employees. Each super-vised employee reports to only one supervisor. Each employee, upon employment, is assigned a unique employee identification number. In addition to the employee's name, position, and ID number, the company also records each employee's social security number, address, and phone.

VINEYARD HOLDINGS AND GRAPE VARIETIES

LVI's vineyard holdings now include ten plots of land, in separate locations, ranging in size from two acres to twenty acres. Each vineyard has its own unique name, such as Hilltop, Westside, etc. and each is managed by a single employee. No employee manages more than one vineyard.

The location and size, measured in acres, of each vineyard is recorded. Each vineyard is dedicated to the growing of a single grape variety per vintage year. However, over time a particular vineyard may be replanted to a different grape variety, depending on market demand for particular types of wine. The winery maintains a record of these plantings.

LVI currently grows six different grape varieties: Cabernet Sauvignon, Merlot, Zinfandel, Pinot Noir, Chardonnay, and Sauvignon Blanc. Information that is specific for each grape variety and must be recorded includes the juice conversion ratio, a measure of how much juice, on average, can be extracted from a given weight of a grape variety. The wine storage requirement, which is the type of storage container (typically either stainless steel tank or oak barrel) used to hold the juice while it ferments into wine, is also recorded for each grape variety, as is the wine aging requirement, which is the measure of how long the wine produced from the juice should be stored before bottling. Certain measures related to the grapes that vary with the specific vintage year harvest are also recorded including the vineyard the grapes come from, the total amount (weight) of grapes harvested, and the ripeness of the grapes (expressed in % sugar).

WINE PRODUCTS AND BOTTLES

Information on the wines created from the grapes must, of course, be recorded. Each wine produced is given a unique identification number in addition to its name. Other information recorded for each wine is its vintage year, category (e.g., dry red, dessert, etc.), and percent alcohol, a legal requirement. Also recorded is the employee in charge of making that wine. Wine makers may be responsible for more than one wine at a time.

The composition of a wine may be entirely from a single grape variety or may be a blend of more than one variety. The proportion of juice from each grape variety for each wine produced must be recorded. Several of the grape varieties are used in more than one blended wine. None of LVI wines are vineyard specified; that is, the wines are labeled by the grape varieties contained in the wines only, without reference to specific vineyard plots.

The wines are sold in case lots. The winery refers to these case lots as products. A product is a specific wine in a specific bottle size in a specific case quantity sold at a specific price. Each product type is given a unique product identification number. LVI does not sell partial cases, nor does it mix wines or bottle types in a single case.

The bottles used for the wines vary in capacity, shape, and glass color. Each bottle type is assigned a unique bottle identification code. LVI maintains an inventory count of how many of each bottle type is currently on hand in their warehouse. The winery prefers to keep at least a month's worth of bottle inventory on hand. The usual cost per bottle is also recorded for each bottle type to aid in pricing the products and as a guide in calculating expected future bottle order costs.

The bottles must be purchased from outside glass vendors. Each of these vendors is assigned a unique identification number. In addition to this number, each vendor's name, address, and phone are recorded. Also recorded, for each vendor, is the name of the principal contact (i.e., account representative) at the vendor that handles the LVI account.

Bottles are acquired from the vendors by placing orders. Some bottle types may be ordered from more than one vendor. Each order involves only a single vendor but may include more than one bottle type. Usually orders are filled completely by the vendors, but occasionally an order must be filled with multiple shipments, due to a back-order condition at the vendor. LVI maintains careful records of what quantities are ordered and what quantities are received, as well as when the bottles are ordered and when they are received, and the actual price charged for the bottles.

CUSTOMERS

LVI's customers are mainly restaurants and wine shops, but the winery also sells to individuals via a mail-order newsletter. All customers are assigned a unique customer identification number and this number is recorded along with their address and phone. Individual customers also have their first and last names recorded along with their date of birth, in order to demonstrate legal age. Restaurants and wine shops have their company name and tax identification number recorded.

All customers obtain their products from LVI by placing orders. Each order is assigned a unique order number, and the date the order is received is recorded along with the product or products ordered and the quantity or quantities desired. A shipment status of "pending" is assigned to an order until it is actually shipped, whereupon the status is then changed to "shipped". Customer orders are always filled in a single shipment, as no back orders are possible. Once LVI is out of a given wine for a particular year, no more can be produced.

CONCLUSION

The preceding information was obtained by an analyst representing your consulting firm through early discussions with Mr. and Mrs. Woods, and observations of the operations of the company. Further discussions with the Woods, as well as interviews with other LVI employees, have since been conducted along with a thorough analysis of the written records of the company. A couple of additional pertinent points have been determined, as follows:

- The database system initially desired by the Woods will not have to handle employee payroll, as this is handled by an external accounting firm.

- No other inventory requirements exist for the system beyond those previously identified. Corks, labels, and packing boxes are acquired in large annual lots and are not a concern for the Woods to track with the database system.

The Woods are hopeful that the database system you will design for them will help take some of the record keeping burdens off them so that they can spend more of their time involved with the grape growing and wine making activities that they love. You and your team look forward to the challenge of developing such a system for LeeAnne Vineyards.

CASE E

An NCAA College Basketball Database

INTRODUCTION

College athletics has caused concerns for many years. Rule infractions at many schools have been widely reported in the press. Graduation rates have been as low as 32% for a final four team in the men's basketball tournament in 2002. Many players exhaust their years at college and end up without a college degree. Concerned about these issues, the National Collegiate Athletic Association (NCAA) the governing body of collegiate athletics could develop a web-driven database application that allows schools to provide the NCAA with data it needs to more closely monitor player activities. For example, schools are required to submit squad lists that qualify student-athletes for intercollegiate competition. The NCAA also obtain academic performance measures such as individual and team GPAs on an annual basis. The application would initially be restricted to men's basketball programs and, if successful, could easily be expanded to other sports. Details of the information requirements for such an application have been drawn from the current NCAA website (www1.ncaa.org and www.ncaa.org).

INFORMATION REQUIREMENTS

SCHOOLS

The initial application would include Division I schools men's basketball teams with the intention that other schools could be added later. Accessing the system via a Web browser, each school is expected to input or verify for accuracy the following data items:

- name of the school
- location (city and state)
- school enrollment
- type of institution (public or private)
- arena name
- arena size indicating the seating capacity of the stadium in which the team plays it home games
- name of the conference (currently about 32 conferences)
- region (East, South, Midwest, and West)
- name of the athletic director
- number of in-state players that are from the state in which the school is located
- number of out-state players that are from out-of state for the three most recent years
- number of scholarships the school offered in each of the three most recent years
- number of infractions by a team that has been brought to the attention of the NCAA. Incidents are represented by 5-digit codes that identify the specific nature of the incident under question.

PLAYERS

Several data items about individual players on each team need to be maintained as part of the database. The system needs to keep track of the player's name (last name, first name, middle initial), ethnicity, date of birth, school name of the player, and month and year the player joined the team. The NCAA also wants to record: the name of the high school from which the player graduated, his high school GPA, date of graduation, combined SAT scores and/or ACT scores, and the number of active collegiate athletes that graduated from the same high school as the player in question.

In order to remain eligible to play, student-athletes must demonstrate satisfactory academic progress in each academic year. Consequently, the database should keep track of the number of hours attempted, hours earned, courses taken and grades in those courses, and total GPA for the total hours attempted. The system should also indicate if a player is enrolled full-time, meaning that the player earns 24-semester hours or 36-quarter hours since the beginning of the previous fall term or since the beginning of the school's preceding regular two semesters or three quarters.

In terms of the athletics, the system needs to track each player's height and weight (to be updated each semester/quarter), the position that the player predominantly plays, and a list of injuries sustained by the player since he joined the team.

Each academic year, schools are expected to submit squad lists by the first day of competition, which provide two types of information about each player: identification and status (including status changes), and financial aid information. Table 1 shows the information about each player that needs to be submitted. Squad lists also list the name and location (city and state) of the school, the name, title, and telephone number of the person who completed the list, and the date the list was submitted.

Table 1: Squad Lists Data Items

General Information	ID Number	for each student athlete
	Name	for each student athlete
	Eligible to compete	eligible (y), not eligible (N)
Student Status	Term first enrolled at any institution	
	Academic Calendar	"Semester" or "Quarter"
	Term and year	(for "Semester Schools": F for fall, S for spring, for "Quarter Schools": F for fall, W for winter, S for spring)
	Term first enrolled at current institution	
	Academic Calendar	"Semester" or "Quarter"
	Term and year	(for "Semester Schools": F for fall, S for spring, for "Quarter Schools": F for fall, W for winter, S for spring)
	Number of years received financial aid	not including the year it is reported
Change in Status	Reason	C (cut or dismissed), E (exhausted eligibility), G (graduated), M (medical exception resulting from career-ending injury of condition), Q (quit the team)
	Date	effective date of the change in status
Financial Aid	Number of seasons used	number of seasons of competition the student-athlete has been used
	Amount of athletics grant	the dollar amount the institution has awarded the player in athletics grant-aid
	Amount of other countable aid	dollar amount of other institutional financial aid
	Total countable aid	dollar amount of the total countable financial aid

COACHES

A team usually has one head coach and several assistant coaches. For each coach, the following data is to be maintained: name of coach, school, title, current base salary, changes in base salary as they occur, hire date, and a list schools and job titles held by this coach prior to joining the team. Salary information is public information in state schools, but may not be available at all schools.

GAMES

An important part of the application consists of tracking data about the games played by each team in the database. A team plays many other teams during a season, either at home, at the other team's stadium, or at a third neutral site. The following information needs to be recorded: names of both teams, game site, designation for each team (home or visiting), attendance at the game, the score for each team, and the number of injuries incurred by each team in the game. In addition, the system should track scoring by individual players per game, specifically the total number of points scored, number of field goals (FG), number of free throws (FT), number of three point field-goals (3FG), and number of assists, rebounds, and steals. Furthermore, with the player foul limit being five, there is an interest in tracking the number of fouls per player per game to be able to compute statistics such as fouls per game and number of players that are fouled out.

REPORTS

Leslie's interviews indicate that the system would be used to generate two types of reports: periodic and ad hoc. Periodic reports are reports that are generated at particular times during the year such as at the end of the season or academic year. There are plans to make some of these available on the web site as PDF files. Ad hoc reports are requests for information from the database at any time and would be generated on the spot. The content of such reports is identified at the time the information is requested. The following reports are needed.

CONFERENCE REPORTS

Several reports need to be generated at the end of each season to track what was going on in each of the conferences and determine if there were significant differences between the conferences. One of the reports would track the win-loss records of teams in the conference, listed in descending order of the winning percentage as shown in Table 2. The report would include the following items: conference name, team name, number of wins (W), number of losses (L), total games played, and winning percentage. Another report should show the average head coach salaries by conference, in descending order of salaries. A third report should provide information about the ethnic or racial composition of the teams in each conference as shown in Table 3.

Table 2: 200xTeam Winning Percentage by Conference

Conference	Team	Wins	Losses	Total Games Played	PCT
Independents	Best	19	8	27	.704
	Second Best	20	10	30	.667
	Third	14	13	27	.519
	Fourth	13	14	27	.481
	…	…	…		…
Far West	Best	19	7	26	.730
	Second Best	19	8	27	.704
	Third	13	12	25	.520
	…	…	…		…

Table 3: 200xTeams' Ethnic Composition by Conference

Conference	American Indian/ Alaskan Native	Asian/ Pacific Islander	Black	Hispanic	White	Other
Independents	0%	2%	55%	3%	40%	0%
Big South	0%	0%	…	…	…	…
Top Ten	0%	…	…	…	…	…
Far West	1%	…	…	…	…	…
…	…	…	…	…	…	…

TEAM REPORTS

Based on Leslie's interviews, interest was also expressed in attendance reports with one sorted by attendance and the other one alphabetically by team name. As shown in Tables 4 and 5, items needed for these report include the school name, the number of games they played, the total attendance, and average attendance per game.

Table 4: NCAA Division I Men's Basketball Attendance (ranked by average attendance)

Rank	School	# of Games	Attendance	Average
1.	Florida University	12	261,435	21,786
2.	California University	14	291,705	20,836
3.	Ohio University	17	327,789	19,282
4.	Mississippi	17	298,172	17,540
5.	...	...	...	...

Table 5: NCAA Division I Men's Basketball Attendance (alphabetically by team)

Team	# of Games	Attendance	Average
Airborne	14	21,640	1,546
Bullets	13	36,332	2,795
CA Univ.	14	291,705	20,836
Chargers	18	187,994	10,444
Desperados	13	19,267	1,482
...	...	...	...

A report highlighting team highs should list the number of points scored by the winning team, name of the winning team, name (and number of points) of the opponent (and points), and the date of the game (Table 6).

Table 6: 200x-200x Team Scoring Highs

Points	Team vs. Opponent (Pts.)	Date
141	Airborne vs. Bullets (92)	Dec. 24
130	Airborne vs. Chargers (71)	Dec. 30
125	Chargers vs. Floridians(50)	Dec. 10
123	Desperados vs. Californians (90)	Dec. 16
...	...	...

Also of interest is a regular season game attendance report as shown in Table 7. The report should list attendance (sorted in descending order), the home team and the opponent, the points scored by each team, the location of the game (arena name, city, state), and the date of the game.

Table 7: 200x-200x Regular Season Game Attendance (ranked by attendance)

Attendance	Home Team (Pts) vs. Opponent (Pts.)	Arena	City	State	Date
29,453	New Yorkers (63) vs. Floridians (62)	Carrier Dome	Syracuse	NY	Feb. 10
23,621	Chargers (84) vs. Californians (74)	Rupp Arena	Lexington	KY	Jan. 16
23,381	Chargers (86) vs. Airborne (75)	Rupp Arena	Lexington	KY	Jan. 27
23,164	New Yorkers (70) vs. Desperados (83)	Carrier Dome	Syracuse	NY	Dec. 22
...	...	...			...

ATHLETIC PERFORMANCE REPORTS

With an eye towards monitoring the athletic performance of players, the NCAA is interested in tracking high-scoring players. The report to be generated at the end of each year (Table 8) should show the number of points scored, the name of the player, the game at which the player scored the points, and the date of the game.

Table 8:   Final 200x-200x Division I Men's Basketball Individual Scoring Highs (by player)

Points	Player	Team vs. Opponent	Date
50	Jack Brie	Chargers vs. Floridians	Jan. 24
49	Nelson Howard	New Yorkers vs. Airborne	Mar. 3
45	Chris Seton	Bullets vs. Chargers	Mar. 6
44	George Friday	New Yorkers vs. Desperados	Nov. 20
…	…	…	…

At the end of the season, final statistics such as the ones shown in Table 9 are compiled for each player. The report should be sorted by average points per game listing the player with the highest average first, but could also be sorted by other characteristics such as the total number of field goals (TFG), number of 3-point field goals (3FG), number of free throws, and total points scored. The player's school, class (SR, JR, SO, FR), and height should also be shown.

Table 9: Final Player Statistics

Rank	Name	School	Class	Height	#of Games	TFG	3FG	FT	PTS.	AVG.
1.	Jack Brie	Outstanding U.	SR	6-4	27	244	85	214	787	29.1
2.	Nelson Howard	Eastern Very Good.	SR	6-2	31	250	86	151	737	23.8
3.	Wayne Good	Good College	SR	6-3	27	216	107	98	637	23.6
4.	George Friday	Good State U.	SO	6-4	30	208	62	207	685	22.8
...	...	...			...					

ACADEMIC PERFORMANCE REPORT

Several academic awards are available to NCAA student-athletes including the NCAA Academic All American and the NCAA Walter Byers Postgraduate Scholarship. The system should therefore generate reports that identify players and teams who excel not only in athletics, but off the field as well. One report should list the top 25 student-athletes, ranked by grade point average (GPA), and showing the name of the school, location of school, and the conference. Another report should list the top 25 academic teams based on their team grade point average(see Table 10). Team grade point averages are determined by the total number of quality points divided by the total number of hours attempted for the academic school year that is reported.

Table 10: Academic Top 25 Teams for the 200x-0x Academic Year

Rank	Name of School	Avg. GPA
1.	The Best University	3.620
2.	Outstanding University of the State	3.594
3.	Excellent State University	3.591
4.	Top State University	3.555
....	....	....

INJURY REPORTS

With the number of injuries on the rise, the NCAA expressed an interest in monitoring the number of game-related injuries in the form of several reports. The first report, generated at the end of each season, would show a listing of each team's total of number of injuries. The second report should identify teams involved in games in which the number of injuries exceeded ten and should list the date of the game, the number of injuries (in descending order), the arena where the game was played, and the score differential. The final report shown in Table 11 should be generated when a player sustained his sixth injury of the season during a game. This report would then be discussed with the player's school to investigate whether the school was taking appropriate measures to prevent injuries.

Table 11: Individual Injury Report

Jack Injured
California University
March 12, 200x

1.	Bruised rib	Jan 3, 200x
2.	Twisted ankle	Feb 4, 200x
3.	Broken wrist	Mar 8, 200x
	...	

REPORT OF FOULS

The NCAA is also interested in reports that indicate which teams and individual players incurred the highest number of fouls during a particular season. According to NCAA rules, a player may not remain in the game after committing a 5th personal foul. The individual players report should list the name of the player, the team, and the number of fouls incurred, sorted in descending order. The team report should list the number of fouls per team, indicating team name, conference, and total number of fouls. A third report should list the number of foul-outs per player, the player's team name, the conference name, listed in descending order of foul-outs.

COACHES REPORTS

Several reports are needed to keep track of coaches' career successes and records. The first two reports to be generated at the end of each year should contain the following information: number of years as a head coach, team name, number of games won, number of games lost, and winning percentage. The first report should be sorted by winning percentage in descending order, the second one by last name. A third report should highlight successful coaches and be generated for head coaches who had a winning percentage that exceeded .60 as shown in Table 12, with the most successful coach listed first.

Table 12: Successful Coaches

No.	Head Coach	Team	Yrs.	Won	Lost	Pct.
1.	Jerry Best	Best University	30	759	187	.802
2.	Roy Second-best	Second-best College	22	539	134	.801
3.	Gale Third best	Third University	17	361	125	.743
…	…	…	…	…	…	…

SOURCES

1. Squad lists are an NCAA compliance form (Form 01-5) that can be downloaded from the NCAA's website at: www1.ncaa.org/eprise/main/membership/membership_svcs/compliance_forms/d1_index

2. Information on squad lists can also be found in the *NCAA Guide to Financial Aid*, available at www.ncaa.org/library/membership/financial_aid_guide/.

3. The ethnic composition report in this case is based on the NCAA's *2001-02 Athletics Certification Self-Study Instrument* downloadable from www1.ncaa.org/membership/membership_svcs/athletics_certification/resources.

4. Other reports are based on the men's basketball statistics published at the NCAA web site at www.ncaa.org/newsfrontF.html.

CASE F

Cellibini Mountain Bikes

INTRODUCTION

Cellibini Mountain Bikes Company assembles premium-quality mountain bikes in its factory in Crozet, Virginia. The company takes great pride in the quality and craftsmanship of their products. It is known for its high-performance frames, which deliver durability and reliability for many years. Since the company's founding by Aldo Celli in 1960, all of its bicycles have been hand-assembled at this single plant. Last year, Aldo turned the business over to his son Frank Celli, an avid mountain biker who received his MBA from the University of Tampa. The company has experienced significant growth of mountain bike sales in recent years – about 70% of all bicycle sales are now mountain bikes. Facing increased competition from on-line bike shops, and customer requests for customized models, Frank and others on his management team consider it a strategic necessity to join the information age and replace the existing paper-based system with a database application to support the company's operations and managerial information demands.

CURRENT OPERATIONS

Cellibini (henceforth called "Celli") offers complete bikes, frames, and parts for four major product lines that allow for racing and riding on virtually any surface: downhill, gravelly bike paths, city streets, or neighborhood roads. Table 1 shows that each product line has several models in many different sizes. Model changes occur yearly, with some models being discontinued altogether and new ones being introduced. Currently, a spreadsheet is used to keep track of model numbers and names by product line as well as their introduction and discontinuation dates.

Celli's bicycles are assembled to order. The sales department receives orders from two types of customers: bicycle shops and retail customers. When an order is received, the shop assigns the order to one of the employees on its assembly work force. The worker must ascertain which components are required for the production of the bicycle using a printed list of the components, also referred to as a pick list. After the worker identifies the components needed, he or she goes to the inventory warehouse, issues a request for the parts, and assembles the bike upon receipt of the parts. Before the bike is delivered to the customer, it is stamped with an individual serial number on the seat downtube next to the crank to uniquely identify each bicycle.

Table 1: Cellibini 2002 Mountain Bikes

Product Line	Model	Sizes
Racers	Kilimanjaro	SM, MD, LG
	Dolomiti	SM, MD, LG, XL
Classics	Tierra Verde	XS, SM, MD, LG, XL
	Trail Explorer	XS, SM, MD, LG, XL
	Night Hawk	SM, MD, LG, XL
	Eagle Pointe	SM, MD, LG, XL
Town and Country	Driftwood	XS, SM, MD, LG
	Tamiami	XS, SM, MD, LG
	Orleans	XS, SM, MD, LG, XL, XXL
	Bluejay	SM, MD, LG, XL, XXL
BMX	Mud Zinger I	N/A
	Mud Zinger II	N/A

When workers are not assembling bicycles, they often work on subassemblies. Subassemblies are groups of components that are pre-assembled, placed in inventory, and used later in the assembly of a bicycle. The wheel is an example of a sub-assembly. Each bicycle has two wheels each of which is composed of a tire and a wheel assembly. A wheel assembly consists of a rim, rim tape, spokes, and a hub. Later, when the bicycle is needed, the subassembly saves assembly time, and therefore shortens delivery time. The sample bill-of-material (BOM) product structure tree in Figure 1 shows how a bicycle is assembled from subassemblies and components.

Figure 1: Bill of Material Product Structure Tree

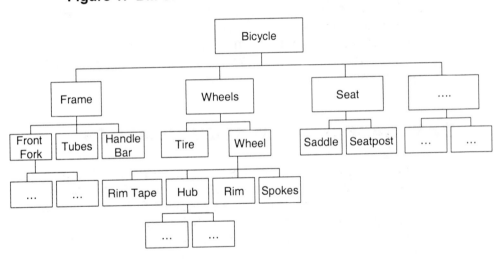

Manufacturing organizations need to carefully plan out the parts they need in production to ensure smooth operations and on-time delivery. While Celli manufactures its own frames, parts used in the assembly of a bike are sourced from a wide range of independent suppliers (e.g., Bontrager, Continental, and others for tires, Shimano, Cannondale, and others for hubs, etc.). Since the company's founding, all inventory management operations have been supported by a paper-based system, which has resulted in occasional inventory problems. For example, orders for bikes have been delayed in the past because parts were not in the inventory warehouse although the accounting system showed them as being in stock. In that situation, the scheduler contacts the sales department so that the affected customer(s) can be notified of a change in the promised date.

Identifying the best components and constantly checking the quality of components received from suppliers are an integral part of Celli's strategy of producing the best bikes in the business. It is not unusual for the company to change from one supplier to another if it is dissatisfied with a current shipment's quality. Part substitutions are currently noted on the diagrams that show how a bike is to be assembled. A separate diagram is maintained for each bicycle model. This paper-based system has led to several problems. First, part substitutions are often difficult to read because of poor handwriting and/or multiple changes for a part. Also, customer requests for customizations cannot be accommodated easily. Finally, when engineering changes are made to the models, each diagram has to be completely redone.

DATABASE SYSTEM REQUIREMENTS

To determine the information needs for the new system, Frank convened several meetings with Gianda Bernadi, VP of sales and marketing, Larry Franco, Celli's shop scheduler, Bob Jacobini, the inventory manager, and Tomasio Biggs, VP of Engineering. Consensus was quickly reached that the new system would need to track:

- Customers and their orders
- Membership of retail customers in Celli's Mountain Bike Club that entitles them to discounts on purchases and other benefits
- Mountain bike product lines
- Bike models and their engineering configurations
- Parts inventory, including part substitutions
- Part suppliers
- Bills of materials for subassemblies
- Actual configurations of the bicycles that were purchased to assist service technicians with repair and maintenance and facilitate recalls
- Employees who take orders and assemble bicycles

CUSTOMER MANAGEMENT

According to Gianda, the following data needs to be collected from its bicycle shop customers:
- Company name
- Street address, city, zip code,
- Phone number,
- Fax number,
- E-mail
- Main contact

For other customers, Celli wants to record the customer's first and last name, address, city, zip code, phone number, and e-mail.

Customer orders can be for complete bikes and parts. Each order has a unique order number. The order date is recorded. The system also needs to keep track of order details such as part number and description, quantity ordered, size, unit price for the item, and extended price, and a shipping address if different from the customer's address.

Celli recently began to sell memberships that entitle customers to lower prices, member specials, and other benefits. Customers can sign up and save with their very first order. Subscriptions costs are $15 for one year, $25 for two years, $35 for three years, and $200 for a lifetime membership (see Table 2).

Table 2: Celli's Mountain Bike Club Membership Plans

PlanID	Description	Cost
001	One-year Membership	$15.00
002	Two-year Membership	$25.00
003	Three-year Membership	$35.00
004	Lifetime Celli Member	$200.00

MODEL CONFIGURATIONS

To facilitate customizations and model changes, the application should have functionality to keep track of the models and their configurations. Tomasio pointed out that customers should be able to custom-configure a bike and choose from different types of frames, forks, pedals, etc. for a given model. That means, the system should be able to create a variety of engineering bills of materials for a model that would then become the basis for the assembly of a specific bike.

INVENTORY MANAGEMENT

A key requirement for the new system is the ability to maintain all data associated with parts inventory used in the manufacture and repair of bikes. Celli also sells many bicycle parts such as frames, forks, saddles, seat posts, bars, stems, pedals, brakes, levers, rings, hubs, etc. to its retail customers. Listed below are the information needs as identified by Bob Jacobini.

- For each part, the following data needs to be stored: part number, manufacturer part number, description, quantity on hand, quantity on order, unit cost, supplier, date introduced, and date discontinued.
- Supplier information requirements are the same as those for retail store customers.
- While the same part can be sourced from multiple suppliers, parts from different suppliers are assigned unique part numbers. A Bontrager crank has a different part number than a Shimano crank.
- The new system must be able to record information about substitute parts including when the part was first used as a substitute and a discontinuation date.
- There also needs to be a way of determining that an inventory part represents an assembly.
- For assemblies, it is necessary to maintain a bill of materials (BOM) or recipe that describes the composition of that part. The system should record which parts are used in the

subassembly, in which quantity, when the assembly was first introduced, and when it was discontinued. The sample BOM in Table 3 shows that Celli distinguishes between front-wheel and rear-wheel assemblies as they may differ in spoke count, spoke pattern, and other characteristics.

Table 3: Partial BOM

Serial No.	C345-68888-098-09KI82002			
Model	Kilimanjaro (KIL1)			
Size	M			
Part No			**Description**	**Qty**
F345			Celli Kilimanjaro Frame	1
	FR987		Celli KI8 Frame	1
	FO987		Celli Kilimanjaro Fork	1
	HA987		Cannondale 6098 alloy handlebar	1
W345			Front Wheel Assembly	1
	T012		Hutchinson Mosquito Tire	1
	WH123		Wheel	1
		RI987	MavicX139, 32 hole	1
		SP239	2 mm spokes	32
		RT987	Rim tape	
W346			Rear Wheel Assembly	1
	T013		Hutchinson Mosquito Tire	1
	WH124		Wheel	1
		RI987	MavicX138, 36 hole	1
		SP239	2 mm spokes	36
		RT987	Rim tape	
...	...	...	...	...

FINAL PRODUCTS ASSEMBLY

The system should also be able to create and maintain records with the details of each bike that is assembled. Specifically, for each bike the following data needs to be recorded:

- Serial number
- Price
- Delivery date
- Order number
- Shipping instructions
- Color(s) of the bike
- Bike size
- Model number
- Employee responsible for assembling the bike
- Parts used in the assembly process.

This information will help service technicians with maintenance and repair and also facilitate recalls.

SYSTEM REPORTS

Two important outputs from the bill of materials are pick-lists and where-used lists. A *pick list* shows the components and particular subassemblies that are used in the assembling of a bicycle. This report is used by an assembly worker to identify the necessary parts to build the desired product and is similar to the BOM shown in Table 3. For each component needed for the bicycle in question, the assembly worker needs to know the:

- Inventory part number
- Name and/or description of the component
- Quantity used in this product
- Some indication of where the part is used in the product

The pick list should also contain information concerning the product being assembled, such as the model name and number, and the bike's serial number.

A *where-used list* explains how a specific component is used in the assembly of all final products and/or subassemblies. This report can serve many purposes. First, the report satisfies the scheduler's need to alert the sales department of possible completion delays. Also, Celli may need to recall bicycles that include defective parts or subassemblies. Finally, this information can be very helpful when considering the impact of material substitutions. The where-used lists should contain the following information:

- Relevant information about the part in question
- A list of subassemblies that use this part (if applicable)
- A list of the models that use this part
- A list of the final products that use the part

In case of recalls, *a where-list* should also include information about the final product including serial number, model number, and customer information so the customer can be contacted.

Further reports that should be generated by the system include:
- A list of Celli's club members, grouped by membership type, and indicating expiration dates (for 1, 2, and 3 year memberships).
- Sales of bicycles by product line, model, and month to identify the most popular models.
- A list of bicycle shop sales, in descending order of sales revenue to identify the most profitable ones.
- Monthly list of items in inventory, grouped by parts and assemblies, showing part number, part description, part type, quantity on hand.
- List of vendors, including contact information and the parts they supply.

CASE G

Conference on International Business Studies

INTRODUCTION

The Association of International Business Studies (AIBS) is a professional association for academics, students, executives, and managers involved or interested in international business. The organization is strongly international in character, with members from over 25 countries. The association's annual conference on international business studies (CIBS) takes place in March. It is hosted by one of the member institutions and addresses current issues in International Business Studies. Several months before the conference, the AIBS invites scholars and practitioners worldwide to participate in the conference program by issuing a call for research papers. Papers can be classified according to broad topic areas or tracks. Submitted papers are sent out for review by other scholars. Accepted papers are published in the proceedings if presented by at least one author at the conference.

In the past, each host institution has handled the paper submission and registration process differently, using a combination of spreadsheets, databases, and manual lists. This approach has led to duplication of effort within and across institutions over the years and has complicated conference planning and reporting. For example, not tying together data on paper submissions with conference registrations made program planning challenging because it was not easy to determine which authors would actually attend the conference. Having data in multiple formats and locations also made the compilation of after-action reports unnecessarily tedious. Furthermore, difficulties arose with respect to compiling consistent statistics that would allow for comparisons over the years because each institution has handled conference related processes differently.

After the last conference, the association decided to develop a database application that would handle paper submissions as well as conference registrations and facilitate the planning and operations of future conferences. Several interviews with past conference chairs were conducted to gather the information needs and requirements for this application that are described below.

PAPER SUBMISSION PROCESS

As indicated above, the association issues a call for research papers to be presented at the annual meeting. While presentations of papers need to be in English, papers may be written and submitted in English, Spanish, or Portuguese. They can be submitted to one of the following tracks, each of which is identified by a unique code:
- Accounting and taxation
- Business and management education
- Consumer behavior
- Culture, social, and ethical issues
- Economic environment
- Human resource management
- Information technology management
- International business and global competitive strategies
- Marketing
- Strategic management
- Supply chain and operations management

Authors are asked to indicate the track to which they are submitting the paper. A paper is submitted to one track. Each track has at least one track chair, but may have two or three track chairs. A paper can be single-authored, or can have multiple authors. Often, the authors of a single paper are from different institutions or universities.

Once received, a paper is assigned a unique ID. The following information is recorded for each submitted paper:

- Author information (last name, first name, middle initial, name of institution, address, country, phone number, fax number, and e-mail)
- Paper title
- Track to which the paper has been submitted
- Up to five keywords that describe major aspects of the paper
- An abstract, which summarizes key points and is less than 100 words

PAPER REVIEW PROCESS

When papers are received by the host institution, they are sent out for review. Each reviewer is assigned a unique ID. In addition, the following information is recorded about each reviewer:

- Name
- E-mail
- Position (e.g., associate professor, professor, dean, etc.)
- Phone number (including country code)
- Institution
- Field in which doctoral degree was completed
- Tracks for which they can review
- Languages in which they can review (e.g., English, Portuguese, Spanish)

A paper is usually sent out to two or three reviewers. Some reviewers receive several papers. The association records the reviewer's assessment of the paper on four dimensions (conceptual significance, practical significance, conduct of research, and presentation of research) using the following values: excellent, very good, good, average, fair, poor, and not acceptable. Furthermore, reviewers are asked to render an overall decision regarding a paper, which can be: accept, accept with minor revisions, or reject. Comments about a paper are also recorded. Author notifications of the decision to accept or reject a paper are sent by e-mail.

PAPER PRESENTATIONS

The conference is organized into sessions where accepted papers are presented. Each session has a unique code (e.g., ACC_FR1 for the first session of papers on accounting and taxation) and a title that describes the theme of its papers. Each session has a session chair who can be one of the authors, or another person who registered for the conference. A person can serve as a session chair for multiple sessions. Papers can only be presented by their authors. A paper may have more than one presenter if it is co-authored. Papers that are not presented will not be published in the proceedings. It is therefore necessary to record: (1) if a paper was presented, and (2) who presented it.

CONFERENCE REGISTRATION

Past conferences have had between 200 and 300 attendees. At least one of the paper's authors is expected to register for the conference and present the paper. The conference may also be attended by others who do not present a paper. For each registrant, the following information is recorded:
- Last name, first name, and middle initial
- Name of institution
- Address
- Country
- Phone number
- Fax number
- E-mail
- Date and type of registration (early, regular, or late)
- Status (academic, student, guest, or institutional representative)

Conference fees vary according to type of registration and participant's status. Some institutions are institutional AIBS members.

Each institutional member designates one institutional representative who can register for the conference free of charge. Sometimes, registration fees are waived for speakers, reviewers, and others so designated. Reasons for such waivers should be recorded.

Free registrations do not extend to optional activities such as workshops and seminars which are usually offered at additional costs. Using the same registration, conference participants can register guests who are invited to some of the social events at the conference and whose name is recorded so nametags can be generated. Table 1 provides registration fee information from a recent conference.

Table 1: Sample CIBS Registration Fee Structure

Registration Options	Fee (in USD)
Early Registration (by February 15, 200x)	$285
Regular Advance Registration (by March 7, 200x)	$350
Doctoral Students (by March 7, 200x)	$200
Guests (by March 7, 200x)	$100
Late Registration Fee (additional fee for all registrants and guests not registered and paid by March 7, 200x)	$100
Institutional representative registration	no charge
Additional fee for Faculty Development Workshop (Except Doctoral Students)	$50
Faculty Development Workshop Fee (Doctoral Students)	$25

Registration is not considered complete until payment has been received and processed by the registration chair. Payments can be made via check, money-order, or credit card. A payment can cover the registration fees for multiple conference participants (e.g., a check from a university for several professors or doctoral students). For each conference participant, the payment amount and method are recorded.

Upon arrival, each conference participant receives a packet with a receipt indicating type of registration and cost, person's status, optional events and their costs, total amount due, amount of payment received, and balance. The new system must be able to generate such receipts at the conference for on-site registrations.

Conference participants who cancel their registrations in writing by the posted deadlines are entitled to a refund. The amount refunded for cancellations received by the deadline is usually 70% of paid fees. It is therefore important to record the date associated with a cancellation, the refund amount, and the date the refund was issued.

REPORT REQUIREMENTS

To facilitate conference planning and evaluation, the association has indicated that the following reports are needed:

- breakdown of participants by country

- breakdown of participants by status (academic, student, guest, institutional)

- breakdown of participants by registration type (early, regular, late)

- number of registrations versus actual attendance

- acceptance rate of papers

- number of papers in each track

- presenters or session chairs that failed to show

- a summary revenue report as shown in Table 2, showing the number of registrations and revenue by registration type/status

- a detailed revenue report that lists the payment of each participant grouped by type of registration and sorted alphabetically by name within each category (see Table 3 for a sample layout of this report

Table 2: CIBS Summary Revenue Report

Type of Registration	Number	Revenues by Type
Institutional	18	$ 0
Special Guest (Fee Waived)	9	$ 0
Doctoral Students	20	$ 2,440
Early Registration	100	$ 22,400
Regular Registration	71	$ 18,460
Late Registration	9	$ 2,880
Guests	12	$ 1,080
Total	*239*	*$ 47,260*

Table 3: CIBS Detailed Revenue Report

First	Middle	Last name	Institution	Amount Paid	Guest	Paper(s)	Comments
Institutional							
...	...	...	...	0	0		...
...	...	...	...	0	0		...
			Subtotal Institutional:	$0	$0		
Waived							
...	...	...	...	0	0		last minute reviewer
...	...	...	...	0	$100		speaker
			Subtotal Waived:	$0	$100		
Student							
...	...	...	...	$200			
...	...	...	...	$225			incl. workshop
			Subtotal Student:	$445	$0		
Early							
...	...	...	...	...	...		
...	...	...	...	...	...		
			Subtotal Early:	...	...		
Regular							
...	...	...	...	...	...	ITM87, ITM88	
...	...	...	...	...	...		
			Subtotal Regular:	...	...		
Late (Preregistered)							
...	...	...	...	...	...	MGT77	
...	...	...	...	...	...		
			Subtotal Late PR:	...	...		
Late (On-site registrations)							
...	...	...	...	...	...		
...	...	...	...	...	...		
			Subtotal Late OSR:	...	...		
Cancellations (.30 of paid fees)							
...	...	...	...	...	...		
...	...	...	...	...	...		
			Subtotal Cancellation:	...	...		
			Total Registration Revenue	$49,260			
			Total Number of Registrations	242			
			Registration Revenue per Person	$203.55			

CASE

Rose Garden Flowers & Gifts

INTRODUCTION

Rose Garden Flowers & Gifts is a small, family-owned flower shop located in Largo, Florida. It was founded in 1989 when owner Michael Rose left Flowerama, his parents' store, to start his own shop. He wanted to build a successful business where customers would return again and again for their flower needs. Rose Garden is located in the Largo Mall and has grown from a one-person operation to one that now employs five people and as many as ten drivers during periods of peak demand. The shop specializes in roses of all kinds, tropical flowers, plants, silks, dried arrangements, dish gardens and gourmet and fruit baskets. They also handle numerous weddings and parties each year.

Rose Garden participates in the Teleflora nation-wide delivery system, allowing it to receive orders from and send orders to all parts of the country. Their business has grown year after year and their merger with Tampa Bay Florist (Michael's sister's shop) a few years back brought them many additional corporate and personal accounts from the greater Tampa Bay area. The Tampa Bay area is nearing 3 million in population. It is composed of several metropolitan areas hooked together by four large bridges. Rose Garden's business is concentrated in Pinellas County, where Largo, Clearwater, and St. Petersburg are located. However they occasionally deliver to other parts of Tampa Bay.

BUSINESS PROCESSES

Since the Rose Garden is a small shop, the flower designers and office manager take orders received over the phone or from customers who visit the shop in person. They may receive multiple orders simultaneously and each order is hand-written on a pre-numbered order pad. The orders are then categorized by delivery date and out-of-state orders are taken to the office manager to be keyed into Teleflora's Dove™ network that connects Rose Garden with other flower shops across the country.

Orders, once taken via phone or received over the network, are sorted into one of several boxes for that day's delivery or for future delivery. Orders for the next day are typically made up during the afternoon when business is slower and are stored in the walk-in cooler until delivery. Orders for future delivery are placed in a "to-be-delivered" bin and, at the appropriate time, the order is pulled from the box, any special flowers are ordered, and the order is prepared

A major challenge in operating a retail flower shop is securing the correct mix of fresh flowers at the time they are needed. Rose Garden orders flowers from its wholesale suppliers on a daily basis. Each morning, the day's flowers are received from the wholesalers by truck and moved into the walk-in cooler. The orders from the day before, if not already made up, are designed and readied for delivery. The delivery driver(s) then pick up the initial batch of orders and begin delivering them to the recipients.

Each order has a ticket with it that contains the recipient's name, address, and phone number as well as a description of what the order contains. A personalized message card is also included with the delivery. The driver obtains a signature on the ticket and notes the time it was delivered. This ticket is then returned to the store to be logged.

CUSTOMER ORDERS

Each order placed is associated with one customer. Usually customers order one arrangement to be sent to one person. Occasionally, a customer will place more than one arrangement at a time, and each arrangement will go to a different location. It is also possible, especially with a large order such as a wedding, that many items will be sent to the same recipient and are all part of one order. A blank pre-printed order form is shown in Figure 1.

If a customer walks into the store and pays cash for an arrangement, no information about the customer is kept. When the customer places an order, the customer's name, address, phone number and credit card information are collected for billing. The recipient's name, telephone number, and address (where the order will be delivered) are taken, along with a description of what the customer wishes to send and any card message. The price and quantity are calculated and the total is billed to the customer's credit card. A separate service called ICVerify™ checks the credit card number and returns an authorization code (approval or rejection) for the transaction. Rose Garden keeps track of which employee records each order.

Finally, in addition to these two methods, orders may be received from another flower shop through Teleflora's Dove™ network. Such orders are placed by customers who call another flower shop, probably close to where they live, and that shop passes the order along to Rose Garden as a third-party. This happens quite often, as customers often call their local shop to have flowers sent to a distant location. Teleflora's networked system makes it possible for orders to be passed to shops in these distant locations quickly and easily.

Using the current order pad, it is not possible to check on previous orders from repeat customers or to look up their address information quickly. Rose Garden feels that a computerized system would allow them to query the database and pull up all previous orders and/or address information and possibly halve the average time spent taking an order. In addition, the information from these orders could then be used to generate mailing labels for advertising and mail-outs to customers. Currently, mail-outs are an extremely time-consuming task.

Orders that have been received in one of the three ways described above are designed and created by Michael or one of his two designers, K.C. or Nancy. The orders are then placed in the walk-in cooler until delivery. Once the day's orders have been made, the designers can work on making arrangements for the store's display case, meeting with clients for wedding consultations, or planning for the following day.

Figure 1: Rose Garden's Customer Order Form

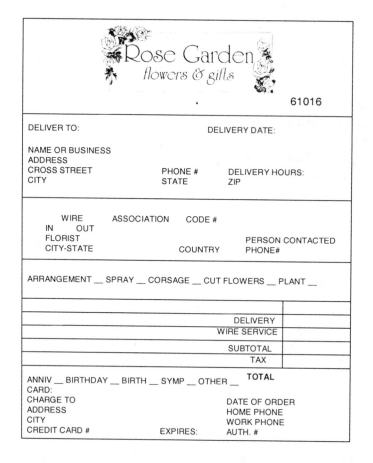

FLOWER AND SUPPLIES INVENTORY

As noted above, during the night and early each morning the Rose Garden receives shipments of flowers from several wholesalers. Some of these orders are standing orders, and come automatically one or more days a week, based on previously established agreements with the wholesalers. Other orders for special flowers were placed the previous day as orders were received from customers.

Michael has certain favorite wholesalers, but he is constantly looking for good deals in flowers. The flower arrangement designers have considerable latitude in the flowers they pick to include in many orders. For example, customers will often specify a bouquet made of spring flowers, with certain colors predominating. Thus, if Michael has located flowers that are available at a good price, he can sometimes buy them in quantity, and use them for particular orders.

For other orders, it is not possible to substitute flowers. For example, an order for a dozen long-stemmed red roses cannot be filled with a fuchsia dendrobium orchid, no matter how good the price on the orchid. Similarly, orders that are placed through the Teleflora system are based on a catalog that all member florists share. This catalog has a number of arrangements, and the flower content of each arrangement is carefully specified. That way, when an order is placed from California, to be delivered in Florida, the customer has a better idea of what is being ordered, and both florists know exactly what is being agreed to provide. Descriptions of some arrangements that Rose Garden makes are described in Figure 2.

Figure 2: Set Flower Arrangements

Name	Description	Flowers	Small	Medium	Large
Spring Fling	Clear vase/assorted flowers	Carnations, alstroemeria, asters, solidaster, stock flowers	35.00	45.00	55.00
Sweet treat	Basket of mixed flowers with candy accent	Roses, orange gerbera, solidaster, soft foliage	38.00	45.00	58.00
Sunshine	Bright flowers in ceramic planter	Yellow roses, orange gerbera, green plants	40.00	47.00	57.00
Rising Expectations	Assorted flowers/helium balloon	Delphinium, snapdragons, Asiatic lilies	50.00	58.00	65.00
...	...	...	...	...	...

Michael would like the computer system to generate pick lists of flowers for each of the set arrangements. He would also like to be able to enter the invoice or bill that comes with each delivery so that he has a better idea of what flowers he has in the cooler. If the inventory is adjusted as orders are taken, it will be easier to know what flowers need to be sold more actively, and which may not be available. Some flowers have a short life span, and Rose Garden would like to improve their utilization of the flowers, based on their life span.

In addition to flowers, Rose Garden keeps an inventory of vases, greenery, stuffed animals, and novelties. These are all included with the flower arrangements, and also need to be tracked. The number of different items stocked is quite limited, although a supply of each of two dozen different vases are kept on hand to use for the arrangements.

Custom arrangements are priced according to size, rather than being tracked exactly by flowers used. The designers have a feel for what should be included in each arrangement in order for it to meet the specifications of the order and still earn a profit. If possible, though, Michael would like to improve his control of the business by being more sure that each arrangement has been appropriately priced and that the flowers actually chosen are appropriate, not only in appearance, but also in cost. He would like to explore the possibilities with respect to automating this process.

ACCOUNTING FUNCTIONS

Patricia, the shop's office manager, handles the accounts receivable and payable as well as the payroll. She must ensure that customers' accounts are paid up, suppliers are paid for flowers they deliver to Rose Garden and employees are paid as well.

The checkbook, along with a daily sales ledger, is used to keep track of accounts receivable. The accounts receivable for house charges include all the customer information (name, address, phone), the date of each invoice, and the total amount owed to Rose Garden.

Accounts payable are also handled in a similar manner and a separate ledger is used for this purpose. With respect to accounts payable, each bill (invoice from a supplier) has its own unique invoice number, along with the suppliers' name, address, phone number, and amount owed by Rose Garden.

Payroll encompasses hours worked for the pay period, wage rate or salary, and calculations for social security (FICA), insurance, Medicare and withholding (tax) to determine net pay. Each employee receives a check and statement of deductions.

Rose Garden believes that a computerized system could handle accounts receivable, accounts payable, and payroll, and would increase their efficiency and save Patricia, the office manager, a great deal of time since she must do all these tasks manually. They have concluded that it makes sense for Rose Garden to acquire Peachtree™ Accounting for its accounting records, rather than incurring the expense of building its own computerized accounting system. However, they have not found an ordering or inventory system that they feel meets the unique needs of Rose Garden.

Rose Garden has contacted your consulting group to consider building a system that will record orders, track customers, generate information about wholesaler liabilities, and handle the flower and supplies inventory. This system will interface with the Peachtree™ Accounting system, which will handle Accounts Payable, Accounts Receivable, payroll, and so forth.

Your team is interested in exploring the possibilities with Rose Garden, and is ready to prepare an estimate of the charges for designing, implementing, and testing a new system for Rose Garden Flowers and Gifts.

CASE

1

Westcoast Floral Inc.

INTRODUCTION

Westcoast Floral, Inc. is a fresh-flower distributor for local florists in the Tampa Bay area. They began operations in October 2001 and have quickly become a supplier to more than fifty retail florists in Pinellas and Hillsborough counties.

Steven Rose, whose family has been in the retail flower business for more than twenty years, started Westcoast Floral to provide retail flower shops in the Tampa Bay market with a large variety of fresh flowers. His goal is to become a major distributor on the West coast of Florida. Steven is well known in the area and he has established a strong client base of customers who order from him regularly. Currently, he has one delivery truck, with plans to acquire additional trucks in the future. His warehouse, located in Largo, Florida, enables him to serve a wide geographical area. The business has been doing well enough that a larger warehouse may be needed within eighteen months.

Steven's new business began with manual record keeping processes, but it is evident that he must consider automating his business processes as quickly as possible. The success of his business is based on his ability to deliver a very perishable product very quickly, and the time required to keep appropriate records and find the necessary information should not interfere with his business of wholesaling fresh flowers.

BUSINESS PROCESS

Retail clients place orders over the phone or in person with Westcoast Floral based on their anticipated demand or special requests from their own customers. They have already begun to request the capability to use EDI in their transactions with Westcoast, but Steven wants to get his basic business processes in order before implementing EDI capabilities. Westcoast's flower orders are mostly placed in response to orders received from their clients because of the fragility of the flowers. The flower importers, most of whom are based in Miami, handle the acquisition of the flowers from the growers. Many of the growers are based in South America, Europe, California and even Hawaii.

Every morning Steven visits his clients' retail shops with his delivery truck filled with the day's flowers. The shops purchase flowers from Westcoast on account or COD (cash on delivery). Invoices are hand-written at the time of purchase (see Figure 1) and brought back to the warehouse where they are keyed into the computer. At the end of each month, statements for each client are printed up and delivered to them, payment being due within 15 days.

Figure 1: Paper Invoice

Westcoast Floral Inc.

000001

9225 Ulmerton Rd. Ste T
Largo, Fl 33771
(727) 584-3734

DATE _____20____

CUSTOMER_____

ADDRESS_____

CASH	CHARGE	C.O.D.	PAID OUT	MDSE. RETD	BAL. FORWARD

QUAN.	DESCRIPTION	PRICE	AMOUNT	

TERMS: Net 15 days. All charges incurred beyond 15 days will be subject to 1 1/2 % interest compounded monthly.

Received By _____

CUSTOMER ORDERS

Order information includes:
- Customer name
- Address
- Phone number
- Products ordered
- Quantity of each product
- Price of each product

The price for the order is calculated and this total is either added to the customer's monthly statement or flagged as a COD order, for which Steven must collect the cash or cash equivalent at the time he delivers the flowers. All customer invoices are entered into a sales ledger, and orders for which credit is extended are added to each customer's balance due. As part of its automation process, Westcoast would like to explore using a digital order pad similar to that used by UPS™ and FedEX™ to enter orders and keep track of customers' purchases.

Since flowers are a perishable commodity, importers and growers often offer batches of flowers at special sale prices when their inventories swell. Westcoast often takes advantage of these sales to purchase large lots of flowers from the importers and/or growers. These flowers are then sold to customers as "Daily Specials" at a discounted price. During certain busy holidays such as Valentine's Day, Mother's Day, and Christmas, Westcoast pre-books orders from clients and, in turn, needs to pre-book these orders with the importers. A computer would allow Westcoast to track these orders and purchases efficiently.

PRODUCT PURCHASES

The flowers that Westcoast purchases from the importers are bought on credit. Westcoast is periodically billed for the product and payment is due upon receipt. Each invoice contains the name of the importer, the date of purchase, a quantity and description for each type of product purchased and the total amount due.

Steven keeps track of each order he places with an importer or grower in a ledger that he calls his delivery ledger. He calls it his delivery ledger because he makes entries in it when flowers are received rather than when he places the order. For example, an order from Tropical Growers, Inc. is shown in Figure 2. A ledger sheet is kept for each supplier.

Westcoast would like to be able to have a report for each supplier's deliveries for the month. Using this ledger, the items must be manually entered and calculated. This can result in errors and incorrect payments to the suppliers. Westcoast would also like to be able to see monthly figures about how many deliveries they have taken from suppliers the total obligation to each supplier and the total still due.

FIGURE 2: Steven's Delivery Ledger

Tropical Growers Inc.
1534 Tamiami Trail
Miami, FL 33122
(800) 555-2357

Invoice	Date	Item Description	Price	Total
46356	3/4/02	100 Wild Orchids	.80	80.00
48295	3/8/02	200 Yellow Roses	.65	130.00
50125	3/13/02	30 Bird of Paradise	.80	24.00
50135	3/14/02	100 Red Roses	.75	75.00
50290	3/18/02	200 Yellow Roses	.65	130.00

Balance Due: 439.00

SHIPMENTS TO WESTCOAST

Westcoast receives their flowers in two ways: by truck or via airfreight. Deliveries of flowers from South America and south Florida are largely handled by the Miami importers and delivered via truck to Westcoast. Flowers from other parts of the world are delivered by air to Tampa International Airport and Westcoast must go to the airport to pick up the shipments as they arrive.

Deliveries that come to Tampa International Airport have an air bill attached that details the shipment contents, the name, address and phone number of the importer, and the total due. Figure 3 shows a sample air bill. The delivery companies also send an invoice for each shipment sent to Westcoast. Similarly, shipments that arrive by truck from Miami have shipping papers attached that detail the same information and the trucking companies also send an invoice for each shipment. Some send monthly summary bills, too.

Westcoast keeps track of shipments received in a payables ledger that contains the shipper's name, address and phone number, date, as well as the product (description and quantity) that was received from them.

Figure 3: Sample air bill

FROM: Shipper Name Telephone
 	
ADDRESS
 	
CITY   STATE   ZIP
 	
SIGNATURE   DATE
	**California
	A ir Cargo**
	
	P.O. Box 354
	San Diego, CA 94035-5672
	(800) 590-4487
	www.ca-aircargo.com
		◎ NFG (Next Flight guaranteed)
		        Prepaid Only
		      Direct/Nonstop Flight #_____
		
		◎ RUSH PRIORITY FREIGHT
		◎ AIR FREIGHT

TO:Consignee Telephone ADDRESS CITY STATE ZIP Printed consignee name	TO EXPEDITE CARRIAGE, SHIPMENTS MAY BE DIVERTED TO MOTOR OR OTHER CARRIER AS PER TARRIFF RULE UNLESS SHIPPER GIVES OTHER INSTRUCTIONS HEREON.	Origin: _____ Destination: _____ Emp. # _____ Emp. # _____ Date: _____ Date: _____ Time: _____ Time: _____

Consignee's Signature _____ Date _____ Initial box below. No hazardous goods$☐

Notify on arrival _____

Comments/handling info _____

SHIPMENT   Declared value _____

# of Pieces	Qty.	Item #	Weight	Rate Charge	TOTAL	Descript.

SHIPPING CHARGES
◎ PREPAID   ◎ COLLECT

Weight charge   _____
Excess Valuation   _____
Tax   _____
Pickup/Delivery
Other charges   _____

Total PREPAID   _____

Total COLLECT   _____

◎ CASH/DL# _____
◎ CHECK/DL# _____
◎ CREDIT CARD _____

◎ KNOWN SHIPPER
◎ SHIPMENT INSPECTED
NAME _____

526 _____9996 2063   CONSIGNEE COPY

Westcoast would like to keep track of all purchases and shipments with a database so they can find out when a shipment or purchase was made, who sent it, and what it contained. Right now the invoices need to be searched manually and it is difficult and time-consuming to calculate end-of-month totals to pay bills.

Steven is very pleased with the start Westcoast Floral has made since it opened and is anxious to continue to provide his customers with prompt and accurate flower deliveries. He anticipates that computerizing his ordering and sales functions will help him to meet his business objectives. He is looking forward to working with your consulting team and to finding a cost effective database solution for his business' needs.

ABOUT THE AUTHORS

Klara G. Nelson is an Associate Professor of Information Technology Management in the John H. Sykes College of Business, the University of Tampa. She received her Ph.D. in information and management sciences from the Florida State University. Her research interests include data quality management, enterprise systems, IT disaster planning, telecommuting, IT implementation, IT and organizational learning, and cross-cultural issues. She has published articles in the *Journal of Global Information Management* and the *European Journal of Operations Management* (forthcoming) and presented her work at many conferences. She has been teaching undergraduate and graduate level database courses for many years. She revised The NCAA Data Base and Cellibini Bicycle Company from the 3rd Edition casebook, and contributed CIBS.

Raymond Papp is an Associate Professor of Information Technology Management in the John H. Sykes College of Business, the University of Tampa. He received his Ph.D. in Information Management at Stevens Institute of Technology and his M.S. in Business and B.S. in Computer Science from Connecticut State University. His research interests include strategic alignment, IT for competitive advantage, distance learning, and pedagogical issues in IT. His recent book "Strategic Information Technology: Opportunities for Competitive Advantage" highlights the use of information systems to achieve competitive advantage and contains numerous cases and research on strategic information systems. Dr. Papp also maintains a consulting practice in Tampa Bay, where he specializes in management consulting, e-commerce design, and personalized computer training. He contributed Rose Garden Flowers & Gifts and Westcoast Floral, Inc.

Weyman Whitlock is an instructor in the Information Systems and Decision Sciences department at the University of South Florida in Tampa, Florida. He specializes in teaching database design and database administration classes. In addition to university teaching, he has extensive experience in software training in the private sector, specializing in database application design and use. He has a Bachelor of Science in Pharmacy degree from the University of Florida, a Masters of Business Administration degree from the University of West Florida, and is ABD in Management Information Systems from the University of South Florida. He contributed Wright Technical Institute, Fit-4-Life, FirstCare Medical Centers, and LeeAnne Vineyards, Inc.